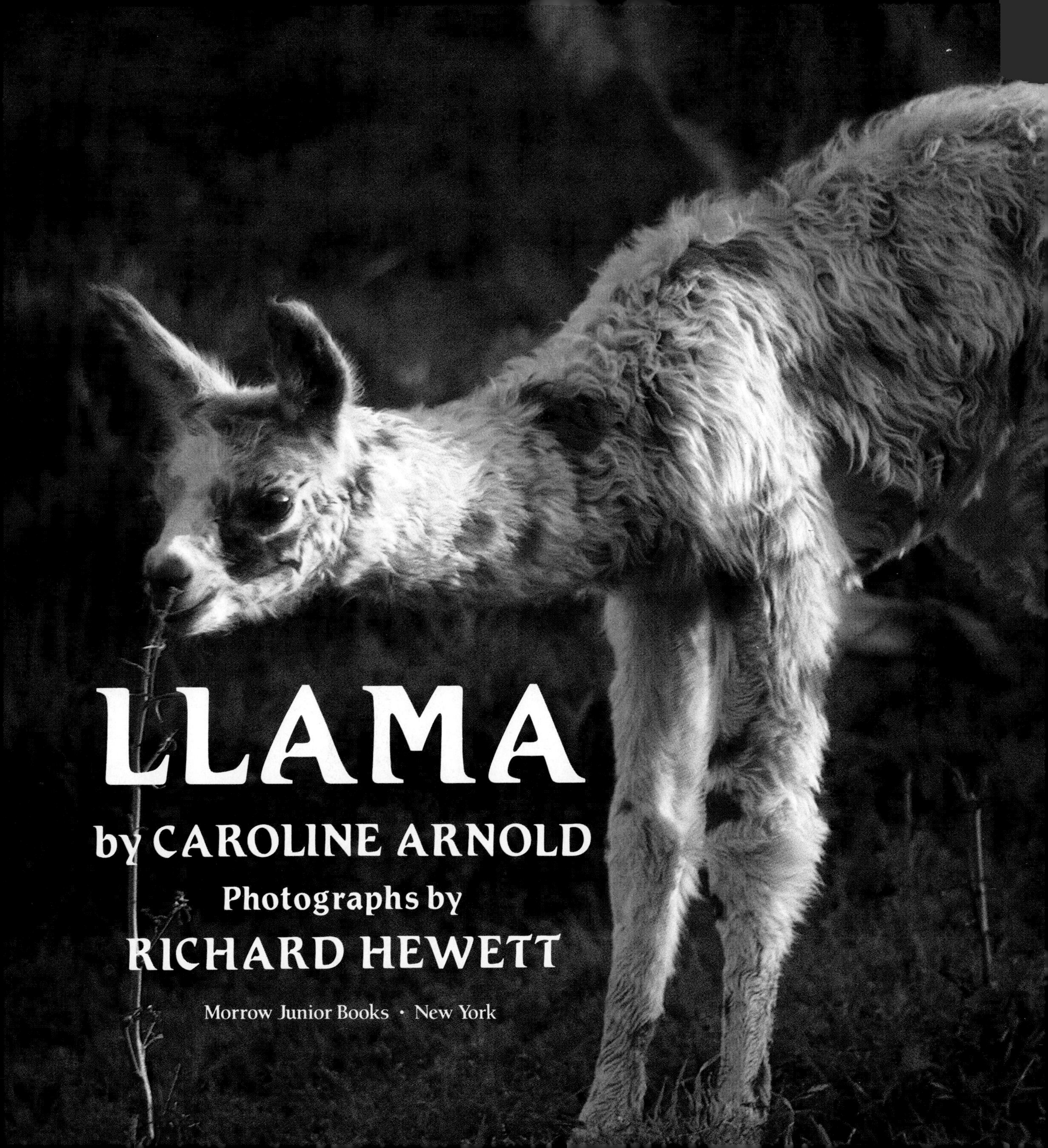

LLAMA

by CAROLINE ARNOLD

Photographs by

RICHARD HEWETT

Morrow Junior Books · New York

PHOTO CREDITS: Permission to use the following photographs is gratefully acknowledged: page 8, Lester Scheaffer; page 13 (bottom), © Zoological Society of San Diego.

 Inquiries should be addressed to William Morrow and Company, Inc., 105 Madison Avenue, New York, NY 10016. Printed in Singapore.
1 2 3 4 5 6 7 8 9 10

Library of Congress Cataloging-in-Publication Data. Arnold, Caroline. Llama/by Caroline Arnold; photographs by Richard Hewett. p. cm. Summary: Describes the characteristics and behavior of llamas and their usefulness to man, discusses other members of the lamoid family, and reports on the growing number of llamas now being bred in the United States. ISBN 0-688-07540-1. ISBN 0-688-07541-X (lib. bdg.)
1. Llamas—Juvenile literature. 2. Lama (Genus)—Juvenile literature. [1. Llamas. 2. Lama (Genus)] I. Hewett, Richard, ill. II. Title.
QL737.U54A76 1988 599.73'6—dc19 87-27130 CIP AC

Acknowledgments

For sharing their knowledge and for allowing us to get to know and photograph their animals, we are extremely grateful to Doug and Jamie Sharp; Jim, Beulah, and Brenda Williams; Art and Shirley Selby; Fred Bauer; and the Steve and Nona Barker family. We also thank Murray Fowler, D.V.M., Maria G. Brown, the San Diego Zoo, and Lester Scheaffer for their assistance. And, as always, we greatly appreciate the support and encouragement of our editor, Andrea Curley.

WALKING confidently on slender legs, the baby llama sniffed the fresh morning air. As she followed her mother across the field, the other llamas gathered around her. They were eager to inspect the newest member of their herd.

The new baby's name was Gypsy. It had been given to her by the owners of the ranch in northern California where she had been born. For the first few days of her life, Gypsy had been kept in the barn with her mother. There it was quiet and the owners could make sure Gypsy was getting enough to eat. But now, at the age of five days, Gypsy was ready to join the herd.

Gypsy and the sixty other llamas on the ranch are among more than twelve thousand llamas now living in North America. About one hundred years ago people began exporting them to the United States from their native land of South America. Today there are llamas in every state and in Canada. They can be seen in zoos and are raised as pets, for their wool, and to carry gear for hikers.

People like llamas because they are gentle and good-natured, easy to care for, and, with training, can become friendly and affectionate. From the time of her birth, Gypsy's owners handled her regularly so that even though she lived with other llamas she would become used to being around people, too.

In the Andes, the mountain range that borders most of the west coast of South America, people have been raising llamas for more than four thousand years. Like sheep, horses, or cattle, llamas are domestic animals. Most llamas in South America today are found in Peru, and their pictures appear on Peruvian coins, handicrafts, and the national coat of arms.

Hundreds of years ago llamas played an important role in the rise and expansion of the ancient Incan Empire, centered in Peru. They were the only means of transportation in a part of the world that did not have horses or donkeys, and they were also a primary source of food, fuel, and clothing.

For the descendants of the Incas who still live in South America, llamas remain a valuable resource. They are used in the Andes mountains to transport goods in places where cars and trucks cannot go. Also, their wool is used to make warm sweaters and blankets.

Llama herd

The llama and its South American relatives, the alpaca, guanaco, and vicuña, belong to a group of animals called the lamoids. They are found on the high plateaus of the Andes. All lamoids are closely related and can breed with each other.

The llama is the largest of the lamoid group and weighs up to 400 pounds (181 kilograms). It is an elegant-looking animal with slender legs, a graceful neck, and a narrow head topped with large banana-shaped ears. An adult llama stands about 5 feet (1.5 meters) tall at the shoulder and 6 feet (1.8 meters) at the top of the head.

Alpaca

Another domestic lamoid is the alpaca. Alpacas are smaller and stockier than llamas and have thicker, finer wool. A full-grown male weighs from 100 to 150 pounds (45–68 kilograms) and stands about 5 feet (1.5 meters) tall at the head. South Americans prefer alpaca wool for knitting and weaving. Alpacas are seldom used as pack animals because they cannot carry heavy loads. Alpacas have also been exported to the United States and Canada and are often kept with llamas.

Today there are no llamas or alpacas in the wild, although they are descended from animals that once were wild. Scientists believe that the ancestor of llamas and alpacas may be the guanaco, a wild lamoid. The guanaco is similar in appearance to a llama but is more slender and has shorter wool. It is also somewhat smaller, weighing up to 210 pounds (95 kilograms). Guanacos are found from the wild mountain plateaus in Ecuador and Peru to the lowland plains of southern Argentina. Like the other lamoids, guanacos rely on speed to escape from danger, and they can run as fast as 40 miles (64 kilometers) per hour.

Guanaco

The llama's other wild South American relative is the vicuña, a delicate, swift animal highly prized for its silky wool. The vicuña is about three feet (.9 meter) high at the shoulder and weighs from 75 to 100 pounds (34–45 kilograms). In Incan times an annual roundup of vicuñas was held to shear the animals' wool. Clothes made from the wool were so valuable that only royalty were allowed to wear them. In recent times the vicuña was hunted so ruthlessly that it nearly became extinct. Today laws protect vicuñas, and herds are slowly growing.

Vicuña

Lamoids are social animals, so they tend to live in herds. Wild guanacos or vicuñas usually live in small groups of females and their young with one strong male as their leader. He will fight any other male that tries to take over his herd.

Most people who keep llamas or alpacas put male and female animals in separate enclosures. This reduces fighting and allows the owners to control breeding. At Gypsy's ranch, young llamas stay with their mothers in the female herd. Males join the male herd when they are about a year old.

Male llamas

Female llamas with newborn

Male and female llamas are similar in appearance, although males may be slightly larger. In Spanish, the male llama is called *el macho,* the female *la hembra,* and the baby *la cría*. These words are sometimes used in English as well.

A male llama is not usually used for breeding until he is two to three years old. A female can begin to breed when she is about a year and a half old and weighs 100 pounds (45 kilograms) or more. She can have one baby a year until she is fifteen years old or more. A female llama gives birth to a single baby eleven to twelve months after mating. Twins are almost never born.

Llama owners often put a female llama into a separate enclosure during the last month of her pregnancy. This way they can watch her carefully and be ready to help out during the birth if necessary.

At another llama ranch, not far from the one where Gypsy lived, several females were due to have their babies soon. Each morning the owners checked the animals to see if any had started giving birth.

One day one of the females stopped eating and separated herself from the others. It was likely that she would give birth soon. A female llama gives birth standing up, and the baby comes out in a diving position, front legs first. As the owners watched, they could see the mother llama's muscles tighten to push the baby out. Soon a pair of tiny feet emerged from the birth opening. In a few minutes the head followed. Finally the rest of the body slipped out, and the baby slid to the ground.

Immediately after its birth, the owners wiped the baby llama's wet wool with a towel. Had the owners not been there to help, the mother llama would have let the baby dry off in the sun. Then the owners applied iodine to the navel to prevent infection. They inspected the baby to make sure that it was healthy and to find out whether it was a male or female. At birth a baby llama usually weighs between 18 and 33 pounds (8–15 kilograms). This was a healthy female llama weighing close to 30 pounds (13.6 kilograms). She stood about 3½ feet (1 meter) tall.

The baby was covered with coarse, curly wool that would eventually grow into a thick, warm coat like her mother's. Unlike her mother's brown coat, the baby's wool was mostly white. It is not unusual for a llama mother to have a coat color that is different from her baby's.

At first the newborn llama rested while her mother stood by quietly. The mother kept an eye on the baby but did not seem to mind when the other llamas came over to sniff it. Then, less than an hour after she had been born, the little llama stretched out her legs and stood up. Although wobbly at first, she gained confidence with each step. Her legs were thin but nearly as long as those of an adult animal. Like the babies of hooved animals, she was able to follow her mother from the day of birth.

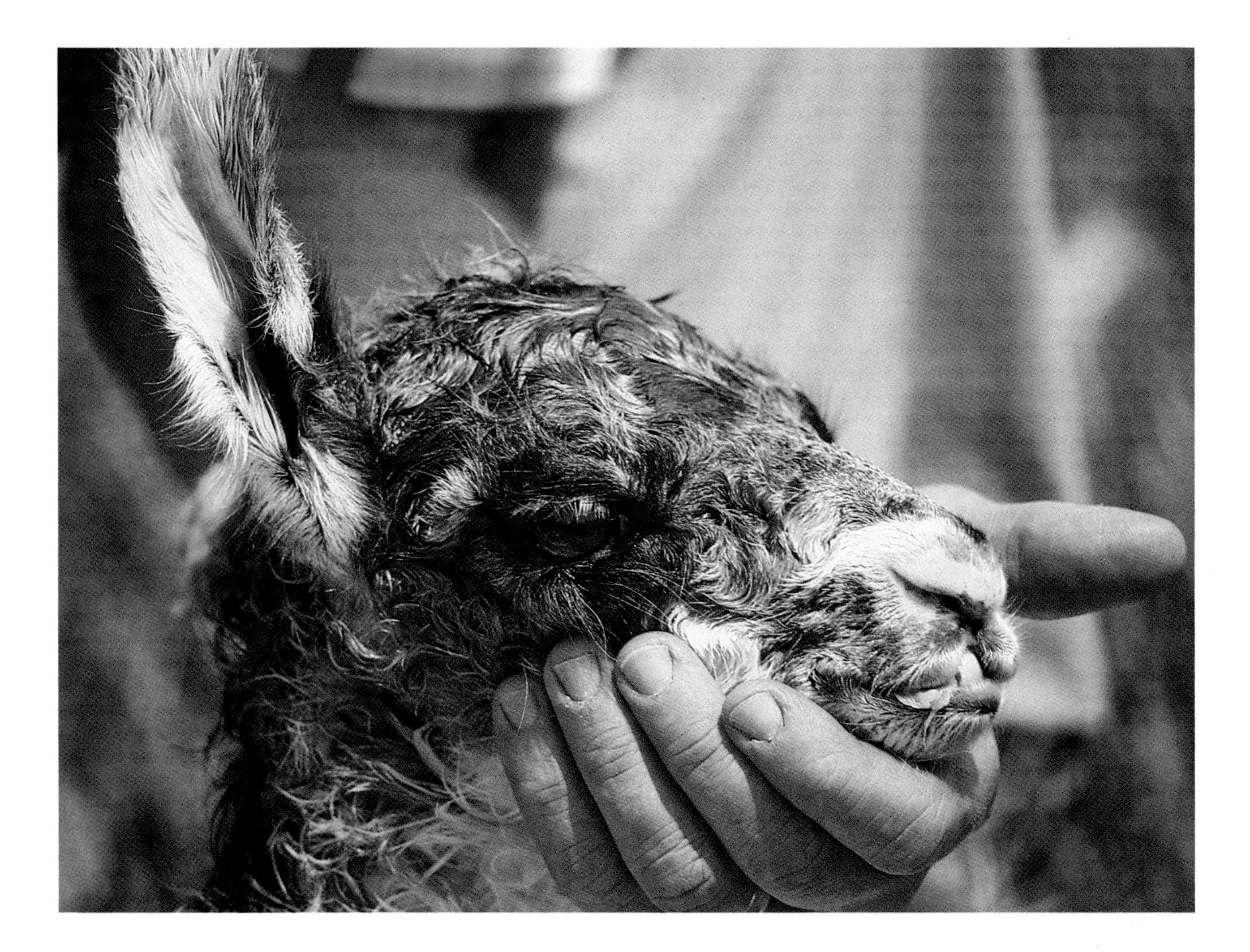

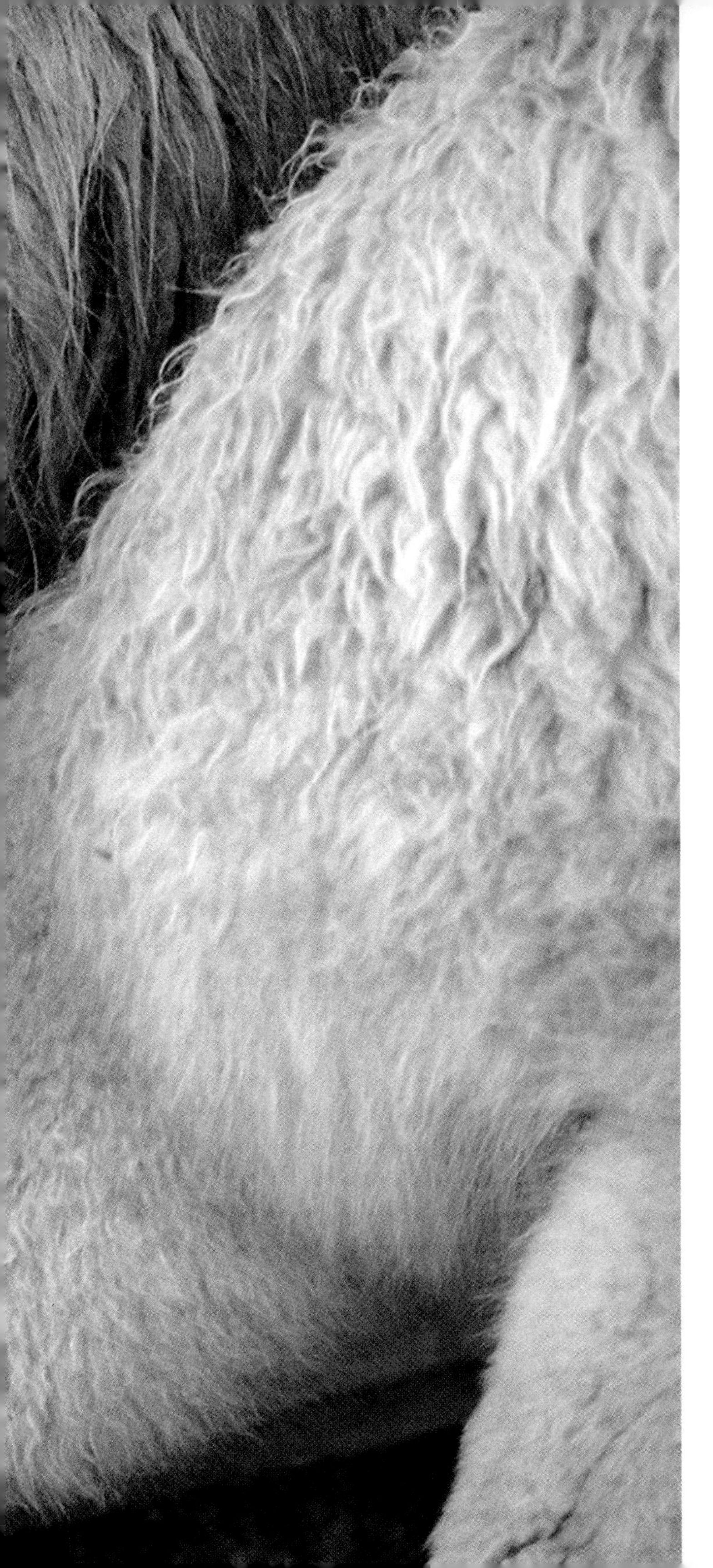

A baby llama's first food is its mother's milk, as it is with other mammals. The baby must nuzzle under its mother's belly to find one of her four teats from which it can suck milk. Milk is a baby llama's only food for the first month. Then it begins to eat grass as well. However, it continues to nurse until it is about six months old. At this age a young llama is about half grown and ready for independence from its mother.

Llamas are plant-eaters. In South America they eat tough, grassy reeds, mosses, lichens, and low shrubs. These are the kinds of plants that grow in the low temperatures of the high plateau, where most llamas live. In North America llamas eat grass and hay. Some owners give them additional food such as grain or minerals.

Llamas have teeth well-suited to eating grass. Like cattle and sheep, they have front teeth only in the lower jaw. These are sharp and good for cutting. Pairs of flat back teeth are good for chewing. A llama also has a flexible upper lip that can reach forward to pull food into its mouth.

When Gypsy was born, her baby teeth were just beginning to come in. By the age of three months, they were complete. These will last until she is a year and a half old. Then they will fall out and be replaced by a set of permanent teeth. All her teeth will be in by the time she is three.

During the day Gypsy's mother spent most of her time grazing, and Gypsy followed her. She was curious about everything around her and often strayed to explore. If she wandered too far, her mother would call her back with a humming sound. When she rested, Gypsy lay down by her mother's side.

The first Europeans to see llamas were the Spanish explorers who came to the west coast of South America in the 1500s. Because the llamas and their relatives reminded them of camels, they called them the little camels of the Andes. Although the lamoids are smaller and have no hump, they are like the camels in many ways and belong to the same animal family, the camelids. All the animals in this group have padded feet, long necks with narrow heads, a split upper lip, and eyes protected by long lashes. Unlike most animals, which have single-chambered stomachs, the camelids have three-chambered stomachs. Food must pass through all three stomachs during digestion.

Like cattle, goats, giraffes, and many hooved animals, the camelids are ruminants—that is, they are cud-chewers. Food is chewed and swallowed, then the chewed food, or cud, is coughed up and chewed again. This is known as regurgitation. Like camels, llamas can go without food for several days because the cuds of food stored in the stomach can be coughed up and chewed later. Unlike camels, which can go without water for several days, llamas need to drink every day.

Llamas use their food so efficiently that little is left over. Their dung consists of small, dry pellets. Because llamas tend to deposit their dung in the same place each time, it can be easily collected and used to fertilize plants. In the Andes, llama dung is also used as fuel.

Llamas, like camels, spit when frightened or angry. When a llama is preparing to spit, it raises its head and makes a gurgling noise. Then, with perfect aim, it sprays the contents of its mouth onto its target. If eating, the animal may only spit whatever is in its mouth. But it may also regurgitate a foul-smelling green fluid from its first stomach chamber and spit this. The experience of being spat upon is so awful that one learns quickly not to frighten that llama again.

Usually llamas spit only at each other. A mother llama might spit at another llama that comes too close to her baby. Males might spit at each other when fighting.

In a group of male llamas, the animals fight with one another to establish which one will be the leader of the herd. Usually the largest and strongest llama becomes the leader. Any llama that comes too close to the leader will be challenged.

In the first stage of a fight, the two llamas arch their necks, flatten their ears, and turn their heads away from each other. The weaker llama is testing the leader by challenging him. Usually, however, the weaker llama heeds the warning and simply walks away. If he wants to fight, though, he lowers his head and looks the other male in the eye. This is the signal to begin the fight.

The leader tries to chase the challenger away. As they run, he nips at the heels of the other llama and tries to bite his legs. A male llama has a pair of triangular fighting teeth on each side of his gums that can inflict painful wounds.

Most of the time llamas make little noise, but during a fight you can hear the males threaten each other with loud screams.

In an intense fight the two male llamas push and shove each other, sometimes rising on their rear legs to butt their chests violently together. They also kick each other with their sharp front feet.

Unlike hooved animals, camels and lamoids have feet with two toes. The underside of each foot is divided in two, with each toe covered by a tough, leathery sole. Llamas are especially sure-footed on rocky or slippery ground, and it is these pads that help them gain a good foothold. Unlike the hooves of horses and donkeys, which have hard soles that crush the undergrowth on back country trails, the feet of llamas do less damage to the environment. For these reasons, they are ideal companions for wilderness hiking.

When a llama reaches its full growth, at about the age of three years, it weighs between 300 to 400 pounds (136–181 kilograms). At this age it is ready to begin carrying packs. Usually only male llamas are used as pack animals. Each animal can carry from 50 to 100 pounds (23–45 kilograms), depending on its size. A llama is particular about how much it carries, though. If overloaded, it simply sits down and refuses to move until some of the load is removed.

Because of the thick wool on their backs, llamas do not need a lot of padding under their packs. Packs vary from cloth bags, baskets, and wooden boxes to specially made nylon packs. Llamas are not strong enough to carry an adult person, although small children sometimes ride on them.

In South America, llamas are used as pack animals until they are ten to twelve years old. After that they are usually killed for their meat and hide. However, llamas kept in zoos or as pets may live to be twenty or thirty years old.

The lamoids differ from camels in that they have developed heavy wool coats, or fleeces. These help keep them warm in the cold mountain regions where they live. Alpacas and vicuñas prefer to live at 12,000 feet (3,658 meters) or more, and llamas prefer to be above 8,000 feet (2,438 meters). Daytime temperatures at those altitudes are often just barely above freezing.

Lamoids have enlarged lungs, big hearts, and more red blood cells to help them survive in the cold, thin air of the Andes. Llamas are well adapted to the high elevations they inhabit in South America, but they have no problem living at the lower elevations where most ranches in North America are located.

The amount and color of wool varies widely among llamas. Some have short wool, with little on their heads or legs. Others are woolly all over. Llama wool can be white, tan, reddish-brown, gray, black, or any combination of those colors. In ancient Peru, pure black and pure white llamas were especially prized. Although Gypsy's wool was short at birth, it will grow longer and thicker as she becomes older.

Llama wool consists of outer guard hairs and a down undercoat. Guard hairs, which make up about twenty percent of the coat, are usually thick, long, straight, and wiry. They protect the animal from wind and moisture. The down hairs are shorter, softer, and wavy, and provide insulation from the cold. Down hairs are preferred for textiles.

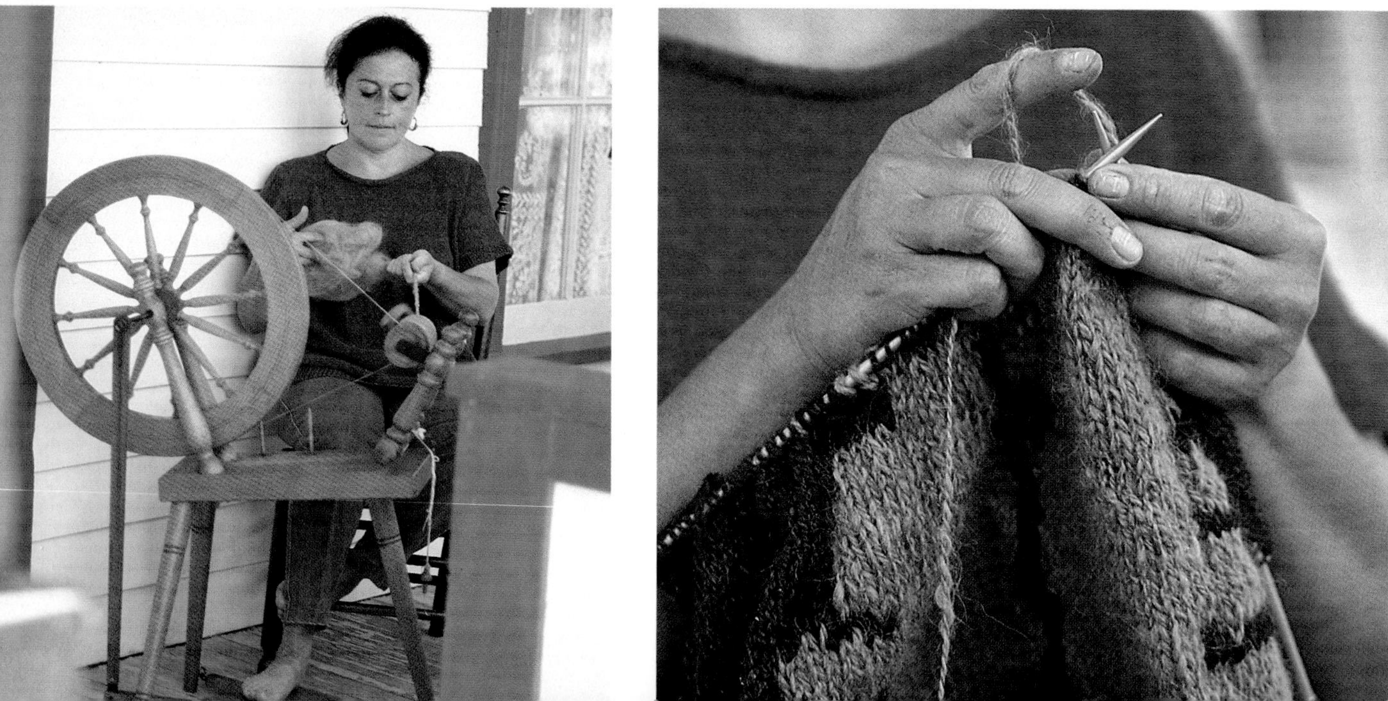

Many people who keep llamas use their wool for knitting or weaving. Although some people shear, or cut, the wool off their animals, most obtain it by brushing. Because llamas like to roll in dirt to keep insects out of their wool, the first step in obtaining wool is to clean the animal. Many people find that the easiest way to remove dirt is with a heavy-duty blower. Then the llama is brushed firmly in the same direction as its wool grows.

As clumps of wool collect on the brush, they are removed and saved in a basket. Later the strands are straightened and made parallel. Any small pieces of dirt remaining on the wool are removed.

A spinner then takes small clumps of the straightened wool and twists them into yarn on a spinning wheel. The yarn can be used to knit or weave beautiful garments. Weavers and knitters like llama wool because it is soft and because it comes in so many natural colors.

As Gypsy grew older, she became more and more independent. She no longer stayed with her mother all of the time. She liked to play with the other young llamas in the field. Like most young animals, the young llamas love to run and chase each other. These games help them to develop and strengthen their muscles and prepare them for life in the herd as adults.

One day Gypsy's owners loaded two of the llamas into a large horse trailer. They were taking the animals to a llama show in Los Angeles. Just as people exhibit purebred dogs, cats, or horses, so llama owners often show their animals and offer them for sale. Llama shows are held in cities all over the United States.

For the two days of the show the llamas were housed in nearby horse stables. There they were fed and groomed for their time in the show ring. When its turn came, each llama was led by a rope attached to its halter.

The exhibitors led their llamas into the arena in groups of five or six animals. The llamas were judged in classes determined by their age, sex, and the length of their wool. Each animal was identified by the number on its exhibitor's back. Walking head to toe, the llamas moved in a circle around the judges. Then they lined up and waited for the judges to inspect them individually. Each animal was judged by standards set by the Llama Association of North America. The judges looked at the animal's bone structure, the shape of its head and ears, the color and quality of its coat, and its overall appearance. The llama judged to be the best was awarded a blue ribbon and a cup.

Because their qualities are those desired by breeders, prize-winning llamas and their offspring can be sold for high prices. On the second day of the show some of the llamas were sold at an auction. Because of the increasing popularity of llamas, some animals sold for many thousands of dollars.

One of the most popular events at the llama show was the obstacle course race for pack animals. In this event each llama and its leader had to run around a course that included going through a small pond, over a fence, and through a row of logs. Each obstacle represented one type of situation a llama might encounter on a pack trip.

Running as fast as they could, the contestants led their llamas around the field. Most of the llamas followed willingly and seemed to enjoy the race, but a few stubborn animals balked. Any animal that missed an obstacle was out of the race. When the first llama reached the finish line, it was declared the winner. As it crossed, the crowd cheered.

As Gypsy grows up, she will be trained by her owners to wear a halter and follow on a lead. Perhaps one day she may go to a llama show, too. When she is ready, she will be bred with a male llama and have a baby of her own.

Young llamas like Gypsy are among the growing number of llamas in North America. No longer do you have to travel to South America to see these elegant-looking creatures. If you like to hike, you might meet a group of llamas on a back country trail. Or if you go for a ride in the country, you might see llamas grazing in a roadside pasture. In some places llama owners have opened their ranches to the public so that visitors can see these gentle creatures up close and learn more about them. As more and more people get to know llamas, the appreciation for these beautiful and useful animals increases.

INDEX

Photographs are in **boldface**.